AMAR CHITRA KATHA

INDIA

A history through the ages

Book 2

The Iron Age

RED
PANDA

First published by Red Panda, an imprint of Westland Publications Private Limited, in 2021

1st Floor, A Block, East Wing, Plot No. 40, SP Infocity, Dr MGR Salai, Perungudi, Kandanchavadi, Chennai 600096

Westland, the Westland logo, Red Panda and the Red Panda logo are the trademarks of Westland Publications Private Limited, or its affiliates.

ISBN: 9789390679270

Text by ACK Comics Studio
Illustrations by Ghanshyam Bochgeri and Zoheb Akbar
Book Design by Ketan Tondwalkar
Printed at Thomson Press (India) Ltd.

India @
75

AMAR CHITRA KATHA

INDIA

A history through the ages

Book 2

The Iron Age

RED
PANDA

INTRODUCTION

At Amar Chitra Katha, the *raison d'être* or the very reason for our being is to uncover the stories of our past. History is not about boring classes or memorisation of dates that others whisper about, warning you to stay awake in class. History, instead, is the magical world of our past. It is a mix of all the worlds that have existed, gone extinct, been reborn and made us the India we are today.

History is the scientific study of the past. The term history originates from the Greek word *historia*, meaning 'knowledge acquired by investigation or inquiry'. A historian is someone who looks through the past.

They understand and organise all the information they can find, and present it to us. History informs us of the past, for a better understanding of our world today.

But for us, at Amar Chitra Katha, history has always been a collection of our stories—a giant library of the past for us to explore. Because we see the world as stories. Stories that bind our civilisation together. They brought our ancestors together on a cold night, under the stars, huddled around a fire, and they are what we all relate to and understand.

In this series of books, we bring to you these stories that will help you in class, for sure. But they are also stories that you will read and love. We hope these books will trigger a true love for history. We also hope that these books will give you a route to your roots. To see yourself through our country's past.

Timeline

1000 BCE To 300 BCE	The Iron Age of India
800 BCE To 300 BCE	Writing of the Upanishads
600 BCE	The sixteen Mahajanapadas emerge

599 BCE	Mahavira is born
563 BCE	Siddhartha Gautama, soon to be the Buddha, is born
527 BCE	Mahavira dies
483 BCE	The Buddha dies

DADI, IT IS SO GOOD TO BE BACK!
YES, AND I HAVE SO MANY NEW STORIES FOR YOU!
I CAN'T WAIT, DADI. TELL US NOW!

TODAY'S STORY STARTS FROM WHERE WE LEFT OFF ...
AT THE END OF THE LATER VEDIC AGE?
EXACTLY!

SO SHALL I CONTINUE?
OF COURSE, DADI! WE'RE HERE TO LISTEN TO THE STORY!
I'M ALREADY IN LISTENING MODE!

MOVING TO THE CITY!

We know that as the *janas* or people came together, they formed *janapadas* or the 'foothold of the tribes'. This was at the end of Vedic Age and the beginning of the Iron Age.

At the onset of the Iron Age, the discovery and use of iron led to a big change in the lives of people in the janapadas. Iron implements were used to clear forests quicker. And there was a gradual shift of the Vedic people, away from north-western India towards the east—leading to urbanisation around the Gangetic plains in modern-day Uttar Pradesh, Bihar and beyond. People found it easier to settle down here, as the soil could be irrigated better, making it easy to farm.

Animals also had larger pastures to graze. Janapadas started to form in these areas. And now, their *rajans,* or tribe heads, grew more and more powerful.

About 2500 years ago, these janapadas and their rajans became more significant. And thus, the Mahajanapadas or the 'great' janapadas were born.

This was the period of the growth of a semi-nomadic tribal society, into an agrarian or agricultural system, with rapidly evolving trade and political systems.

SOURCES

THIS WAS A PERIOD OF GREAT INTELLECTUAL ACTIVITY IN INDIA. THERE WAS A LOT OF FREE THINKING GOING ON!

This period gave us some of the most important Hindu texts. Some of these are:

- **The Upanishads:** Also known as the *Vedanta* (or the 'last chapters of the Vedas'), the Upanishads can be seen as a continuation of the Vedas. Upanishad comes from the Sanskrit words *upa,* or 'by', and *ni-sad,* or 'sit down'. Therefore Upanishads literally means 'to sit near'. There are 108 known Upanishads, and of these, the first 12 are the oldest and the most important. These are known as the *mukhya* or the main Upanishads. While the Vedas, as you saw, talk more of the rituals and systems of Hindu life, the Upanishads are spiritual texts that concentrate more on the philosophy of life, being and the soul.

- **The Puranas:** The collection of texts that primarily collect legends, folktales and traditional stories are known as Puranas. These are stories of incredibly varied topics—from cosmology, lists and stories of gods, goddesses, heroes and kings, gurus and sages, science and technology, astronomy, love stories and even funny stories. Many of these are named after major Hindu deities like Brahma, Vishnu, Shiva and Shakti. There are over 40,000 verses in the Puranas.

■ **The Sutras:** To study the Vedas, you must read the Upanishads and the *sutras*. The sutras are short statements that talk about the truths and rules of various subjects, including, broadly, *siksha* or pronunciation, *chandas* or meter of verses, *vyakarana* or grammar, *nirukta* or explanation of difficult words, *jyotisha* or astronomy, and *kalpa* or rituals. Each Indian religion has its own sutras, as do Buddhists and Jains who hold their own sutras dear.

■ **The Epics:** We spoke briefly about the Ramayana and the Mahabharata in the later Vedic Period, in the first book. But it was in the Iron Age, that the two epics grew into the stories they are remembered for today. Remember, these were all oral stories—stories passed down over time from person to person and not written down. Historians believe significant parts of both the Ramayana and Mahabharata evolved in the period of the Mahajanapadas.

The Iron Age was a time of great discourse and debate amongst people as well. This was a period where scholars, thinkers and philosophers flourished across the region. Scholars would be invited to gurukuls and towns to debate their theories and ideas, and huge crowds would gather to listen to these debates. Winners would get the most prized possession of the time—cows or land. Special halls were constructed for this purpose—the *kautuhala sabhas,* literally, halls that arouse curiosity.

The people of the time were encouraged to build on the works of scholars. These intellectuals would question everything, from the varna system to the existence of gods and goddesses.

POLITICAL AND SOCIAL STRUCTURES

The rajans built cities and palaces with enormous fortifications—huge walls were made of wood, brick or stone. Thousands and lakhs of people lay bricks and stone. These forts were for protection against other rajans invading lands. But they were also to show the power of the rajan and his wealth.

Rajans also began gathering large armies. These were men ready for battle and were paid and maintained by the raja through the year. We see the evidence and growth of trade in coins at this

time, and for the first time in Indian history. All of this required tremendous amounts of resources. Rajans used to get tributes or gifts from their people, and they were already wealthy. However, they needed to find more ways to raise more funds.

So, the rajans started taxing their people. Farmers were made to pay a sixth of their produce. Craftspeople would have to set aside a day every month to produce things for the king or offer an equivalent amount of product. Herders were made to pay in the form of animals or milk, and hunter-gatherers were supposed to give a share of their collections to the king. Goods and items sold were taxed as well, just like today!

But it wasn't all kingdoms and princes, at the Mahajanapadas. At least two Mahajanapadas were ruled directly by the people, in the form of republics or *gana-rajya* or *gana-sangha,* where an assembly of leaders ruled the people.

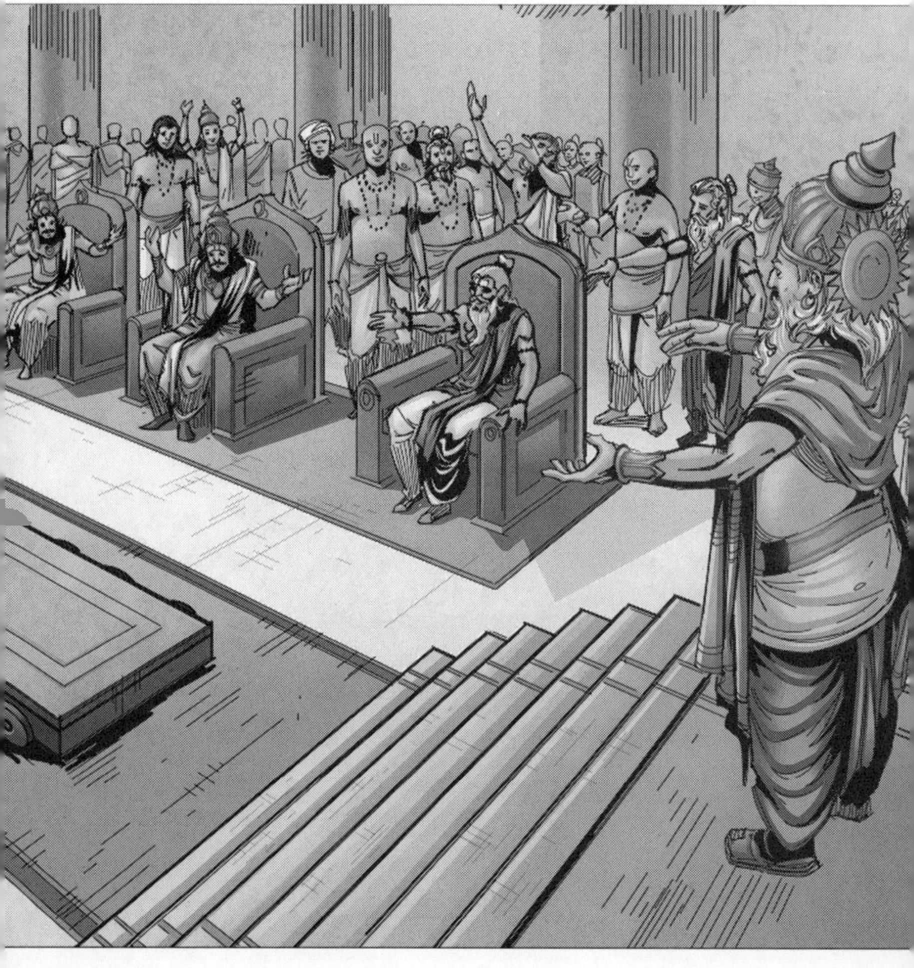

This was also a time of great advancement of agriculture. Iron smelting had become a major occupation, and iron mines thrived. So, farmers adopted the iron plough, leading to a much better yield. Iron became all-pervasive across crafts, furniture, art and technology across the era.

QUIZ

1) Why did the rajans have to raise money through taxes?
2) Can you list what a farmer, a herder, a craftsperson and a hunter-gatherer were supposed to pay to the king?
3) What was the main instrument that brought about great advancement in agriculture at this time?

REFLECT

Can you single out the one most important thing for development of the Iron Age people? Was it the iron plough? Was it the mines? Or was it the changing and evolving political structure?

BUDDHISM

KIDS, YOU MUST HAVE HEARD ABOUT THE PHRASE, 'WHAT GOES AROUND, COMES AROUND.'

This phrase is related to the term karma, which states that every action has a consequence at some point in life. Karma also happens to be one of the central beliefs in one of the oldest religions in the world.

With over 520 million followers all over the world, Buddhism is the fourth-largest religion in the world. It revolves around the teachings of Gautama Buddha. Technically, Gautama Buddha never claimed to be a prophet or a God. This means that Buddhism can exist without the Buddha as the religion basically follows the path to enlightenment that he found and shared with the world.

The religion covers a variety of traditions, beliefs and spiritual practices. There are two major branches of Buddhism. They are *Theravada,* roughly translating to 'The School of Elders' and *Mahayana,* which translates to 'The Great Vehicle.' Mahayana is the most practised branch of Buddhism. Theravada is the second most practised branch, and it is mainly common in Southeast Asia. There is also Tibetan Buddhism which branched out from Mahayana. It is mostly practised in Tibet and Bhutan.

So, who is Gautama Buddha?

He is the founder of Buddhism. He wandered from place to place preaching his learnings. Eventually, he built a family of disciples. His teachings and practices were unheard of at the time. He rejected the caste system and was against religious rituals, priests and animal sacrifices.

There is a lot of evidence in canonical texts that describe Buddha's spiritual qualities. They mention that he was perfectly self-awakened, had higher knowledge and ideal conduct, was very well-spoken, knew of many worlds, was the blessed one, and he was a teacher of both gods and humans alike.

CHILDHOOD

SIDDHARTHA GAUTAMA WAS BORN APPROXIMATELY IN THE YEAR 563 BCE, IN LUMBINI, IN MODERN-DAY NEPAL. THE WORD SIDDHARTHA MEANS 'ONE WHO HAS ACHIEVED HIS PURPOSE.'

Siddhartha was born to Suddhodana, chieftain of the Sakya clan of Kapilavastu and Queen Maya.

When he was born, eight wise men were summoned by Suddhodana. Seven of them made the same prediction, 'O Great King, if the Prince chooses to follow the path of the throne, he will become a universal monarch. However, if he renounces the throne, he will go on to become the Supreme Enlightened One.'

The eighth wise man was more definitive. He said, 'O King, one day this prince will go in search of truth and become the Supreme Enlightened Buddha.'

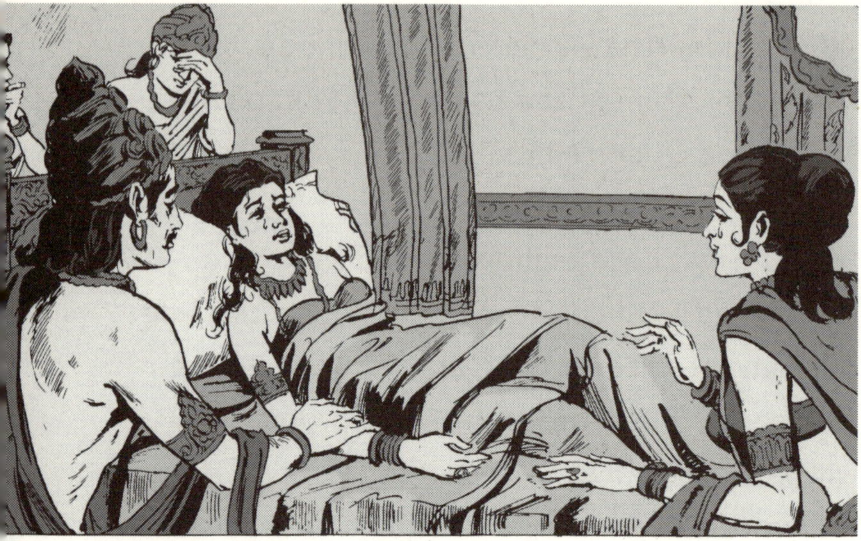

Siddhartha's mother, Queen Maya, passed away on the seventh day after his birth.

King Suddhodana made sure that Siddhartha received the best education and upbringing. However, he did not wish for him to abandon the legacy of the throne and seek answers to the big questions as the wise men had predicted. To make sure that did not happen, he forbade Siddhartha from exposing himself to anything disturbing that might make him renounce his royal life.

So, Siddhartha's life revolved around the royal palace. All the lessons that he learnt were done so within the palace. He was not allowed to go to the gurukul or make friends. Siddhartha grew up alone.

One morning, after finishing his lessons, Siddhartha was playing in the palace's garden when a flock of swans were gliding above in the sky. It was a beautiful sight, but it was short-lived. He suddenly heard a sharp sound and saw one of the swans descend onto the ground. The swan was bleeding and in pain.

Siddhartha ran towards the swan. When he found it, he realised that an arrow had pierced into one

of the swan's wings. He immediately removed the arrow from the wing and whispered to swan gently, 'Here, I've removed it. Let's see how we can fix your wing.'

He then rushed to the garden and gathered some herbs. He made a soothing paste using them and applied it on the swan's wound. The swan looked relieved. Then, he tore off a piece of his garment and wrapped the swan with it.

Suddenly, someone from behind shouted, 'SIDDHARTHA! THAT SWAN IS MINE! GIVE IT TO ME THIS INSTANT!' It was his cousin, Devadutta, his face furious, staring at Sidhartha in anger. He thought Siddhartha was stealing his hunt.

However, Siddhartha was adamant. He looked back at Devadutta with determination as he carried the wounded swan and stood up. He said, 'NO! This beautiful bird has the right to roam freely in the skies where it belongs. You cannot claim its life.' Devdutta was taken aback by the stubbornness of his kind cousin.

He said, 'Foolish Siddhartha! Are you unfamiliar with the laws of our land? A hunter who successfully shoots the animal has the rightful claim over his shot.'

Siddhartha did not care. He said, 'I am as familiar with the laws of our land as you are, cousin. However, since this swan is not dead, it still has the right to life. I just want to help it recover.'

Then, very calmly, Siddhartha proceeded to the palace with the swan.

This made the hot-tempered Devadutta quite angry. He was accompanied by his friends, who were also hunting with him. He said, 'Now that my friends are here, they shall vouch that it was I who shot down that bird.'

The boys were ready to vouch for Devadutta. However, Siddhartha said, 'Save your energy, boys. I am not saying that Devadutta didn't shoot the swan.'

He then thought for a while and said, 'I have an idea. Let's go to the court and let our wise ministers decide the fate of this bird. Is that fair?' Devadutta agreed, and the boys headed straight to the court.

At the court, the ministers were already engaged in several discussions. Devadutta, Siddhartha and the swan in his hand quickly caught their attention. Devadutta joined his hands and in a courteous and respectful manner, addressed the wise men, 'O wise men, we seek thy divine knowledge. Please listen to our dispute.'

The wise men were perplexed. It is not every day that two young boys come to seek justice. One of the ministers asked them, 'How important is your issue that it could only be solved in the royal court?'

Devadutta then began making his plea. He said, 'I shot the swan that you see in Siddhartha's arms. Doesn't that make it mine?'

The ministers agreed and said, 'Most certainly it does. As per the law of our land, an individual has the rightful claim over an animal he has shot.' Devadutta had a visible grin on his face. He knew that he was going to win this dispute.

'However,' said Siddhartha, 'that law is only applicable if the animal is dead, right? In this case, the swan is merely injured. I just want to fix its wing and let it soar in the skies again. After all, doesn't every animal has the right to live?' There was visible confusion amongst the ministers because they knew that Siddhartha wasn't wrong either.

Siddhartha's father, the King, was observing this dispute quietly. However, since Siddhartha was his son, he felt that he had to intervene. He said, 'Earlier today, I came across a wise old man. I think his wisdom would be beneficial to this dispute. Let us ask for his opinion.'

The old man was standing right next to the King. His face was glowing with the wisdom of decades.

The old man came forward and, in a soft, gentle voice, he said, 'Your Majesty, The Prince is right. This swan deserves to be free and live its life as much as any other swan in the sky. Does it not have a family? Should he not go back to them? No one can claim ownership over another being. Prince Siddhartha wants to fix the swan's broken wing and let it go back to its flock. I believe the swan should stay with the Prince.'

Everyone listened to the old man attentively. The ministers discussed amongst themselves and then said, 'Your Majesty, we agree with this man. The swan should stay with the Prince!'

Finally, the King gave the final verdict. Siddhartha was filled with joy. Devadutta quietly left with defeat on his face.

After a few weeks, the swan was fully healed and was ready to go back. Siddhartha smiled and said to it, 'Goodbye, my friend. The time has come for you to rejoin your companions.' Siddhartha noticed two more swans had come to lead their friend back home. The swans flew into the sunset happily.

THE QUEST FOR TRUTH

ONE DAY, SIDDHARTHA WITNESSED A SICK, OLD MAN AND A FUNERAL PROCESSION. HE WAS TOUCHED BY THE CONSTANT PAIN AND SUFFERING IN THE WORLD AND WANTED TO KNOW MORE. HE TRIED TO GET AT THE CENTRE OF IT AND UNDERSTAND THE TRUE MEANING BEHIND LIFE AND DEATH. THUS, AT THE AGE OF TWENTY-NINE, SIDDHARTHA GAUTAMA DISCARDED THE THRONE AND LEFT HIS FAMILY TO VENTURE OUT INTO THE JOURNEY TOWARDS ENLIGHTENMENT. AS IT WOULD TURN OUT, THE EIGHTH WISE MAN'S PROPHECY WAS COMING TRUE!

THIS IS THE STORY OF HOW SIDDHARTHA GOT ENLIGHTENED. BY THIS TIME, HE WAS MARRIED AND HAD A CHILD, BUT HIS MIND WANDERED. HE WANTED TO SEE THE WORLD FOR HIMSELF.

ONE DAY...
FATHER, I WOULD LIKE TO GO OUT OF THE PALACE AND SEE MORE OF THE WORLD.
I WILL ORDER A CHARIOT FOR YOU. AFTER IT IS READY, YOU CAN GO OUT IN IT.

A FEW DAYS LATER, IN A BEAUTIFUL CHARIOT WITH FOUR HORSES DRIVEN BY CHANNA, SIDDHARTHA DROVE THROUGH THE STREETS OF THE CITY.
HOW HANDSOME THE PRINCE IS.
I HAVE HEARD, HE IS BRAVE AND FEARLESS.

IN THE CITY, KING SUDDHODANA HAD ORDERED ALL SIGHTS OF UNHAPPINESS TO BE KEPT AWAY FROM SIDDHARTHA. BUT AS HE DROVE FURTHER–
CHANNA, WHO IS THIS? HIS HEAD IS WHITE. HE SEEMS VERY WEAK. HIS SKIN IS WRINKLED.
HE IS AN OLD MAN, MASTER! HE IS BENT WITH AGE.
DOES EVERYONE GET OLD, CHANNA?
YES, MY LORD! EVERYONE HAS TO GROW OLD.
WILL MY YASHODHARA ALSO GROW OLD? WILL MY STRENGTH GO AWAY WITH YEARS?
ON ANOTHER DAY–
WHAT IS THE MATTER WITH THIS MAN?
HE IS ILL, MY LORD! HE IS CRYING WITH PAIN.
IS DISEASE PECULIAR TO HIM?
NO, MY LORD! ANYONE MAY FALL ILL IN HIS LIFETIME.

EVEN I?
YES, MASTER, EVEN YOU.
STILL ANOTHER DAY—
WHY ARE THEY CARRYING THAT MAN, CHANNA?
HE IS DEAD, MY LORD!
IS HE THE ONLY DEAD MAN? OR DO OTHERS ALSO DIE?
EVERYONE WHO IS BORN, HAS TO DIE SOME DAY.
I FEEL SICK, CHANNA. LET US RETURN TO THE PALACE.
ON THE WAY BACK—
STOP, CHANNA! WHO IS THAT? HE LOOKS CALM AND DIFFERENT FROM ALL THE OTHER MEN I HAVE SEEN.
HE IS A SAINT. HE HAS GIVEN UP A LIFE OF PLEASURE AND PAIN IN SEARCH OF TRUTH.

AT THE PALACE–
SIDDHARTHA! PLEASE TELL ME THE CAUSE OF YOUR UNHAPPINESS!
MOTHER, I HAVE LEARNT THAT ALL THINGS ALIVE AND BEAUTIFUL KEEP CHANGING. MEN GROW OLD. MEN FALL ILL AND DIE. I FEEL UN-HAPPY WHEN I THINK OF THESE THINGS.
IN THE MIDDLE OF THE NIGHT, HE MADE THE DECISION.
I MUST FIND A WAY TO END SORROW. I WILL GO IN SEARCH OF TRUTH, LIKE THAT SAINT.
CHANNA GET MY HORSE READY! I WISH TO RIDE OUT.
YES, MASTER!
BEFORE LEAVING, THE PRINCE RETURNED TO THE BEDROOM OF HIS WIFE. YASHODHARA AND THE CHILD, RAHULA, WERE FAST ASLEEP.
I CAN'T KISS RAHULA GOODBYE; THAT WILL AWAKEN YASHODHARA. I MUST GO.

SIDDHARTHA MOUNTED HIS HORSE AND RODE OUT, ACCOMPANIED ONLY BY CHANNA.
ONCE THEY WERE OUTSIDE THE CITY, SIDDHARTHA GOT DOWN FROM THE HORSE.
CHANNA, TAKE ALL MY JEWELS AND RETURN TO KAPILAVASTU.
HE THEN CUT OFF HIS LONG HAIR AND WALKED ALONE.
LATER HE SAW A BEGGAR.
HALT, MY GOOD MAN! TAKE MY CLOTHES. AND GIVE ME YOURS.
WITH PLEA-SURE, MASTER.
SOON HE REACHED RAJAGRIHA, THE CAPITAL OF MAGADHA. HE WENT FROM HOUSE TO HOUSE SILENTLY WAITING TILL THE PEOPLE OFFERED HIM FOOD. KING BIMBISARA OBSERVED HIM FROM HIS PALACE.
LOOK AT THAT SAINT. HE LOOKS SO HANDSOME. FIND OUT WHO HE IS.

AS SOON AS THE MESSENGERS BROUGHT NEWS ABOUT SIDDHARTHA, KING BIMBISARA WENT TO MEET HIM.
YOU SEEM TO BELONG TO A NOBLE FAMILY. YOUR HAND SHOULD NOT HOLD A BEGGING BOWL, BUT THE REINS OF AN EMPIRE. I WILL GIVE YOU A HIGH POSITION IN MY KINGDOM. COME.

O KING, YOU ARE KIND. BUT I CANNOT ACCEPT YOUR INVITATION. I FEEL THAT LIFE IS FULL OF SORROW. I WISH TO FIND A WAY TO END ALL SORROW.
IF THAT IS YOUR WISH, I PRAY THAT YOU FIND IT. PLEASE COME AND TEACH ME WHEN YOU HAVE FOUND THE SOLUTION.

FROM RAJAGRIHA, SIDDHARTHA WENT IN SEARCH OF THE GREAT SAGES OF THOSE DAYS. NOT SATISFIED WITH THEIR TEACHINGS, HE ENTERED THE THICK JUNGLES OF URUBILVA, NEAR GAYA OF TODAY.

THERE WERE FIVE HERMITS IN THE JUNGLES OF URUBILVA.
THIS MAN IS KEEN ON HIS GOAL. HE IS SURE TO SUCCEED. LET US WAIT ON HIM.
SIDDHARTHA DRANK ONLY WATER AND ATE ONLY FRUITS AND HERBS. HE SLEPT ON THE HARD GROUND. AFTER SOME TIME HE STARTED EATING ONLY ONE HEMP GRAIN EVERY DAY. THIS MADE HIM VERY WEAK. ONE DAY, WHEN HE HAD GONE TO BATHE IN THE RIVER_
I FEEL WEAK. I DON'T HAVE STRENGTH TO GET UP.
HE CAUGHT HOLD OF A LOW BRANCH OF A TREE AND RAISED HIMSELF WITH ITS SUPPORT.

BUT AS HE BEGAN TO WALK AWAY FROM THE BANK, HE FELT WEAK AND FELL DOWN.
SLOWLY HE GOT UP.
NEXT DAY, AS HE SAT BENEATH A BANIAN TREE, SUJATA, DAUGHTER OF A HERDSMAN, CAME TO THAT SPOT. SHE OFFERED FOOD TO BUDDHA.
THANK YOU FOR FEEDING ME.
LATER—
HOW IS IT THAT YOU HAVE STARTED EATING FOOD AGAIN?
I HAVE COME TO BELIEVE THAT STARVING DOES NOT HELP IN REACHING THE TRUTH.
THE FIVE ASCETICS WERE DISAPPOINTED.
HE DOES NOT DESERVE OUR RESPECT.
YES, HE WANTS THE PLEASURES OF LIFE.

SIDDHARTHA NOW LIVED A LONELY LIFE.
THEY HAVE LEFT ME. LET THEM GO. BUT STARVING THE BODY IS NOT GOING TO HELP. I AM NOW SURE OF THAT.
HE MOVED TOWARDS A BODHI TREE AND SAT BENEATH IT.
HEAT AND COLD, HUNGER AND THIRST TROUBLED HIM. RAIN LASHED ON HIM.
COME WHAT MAY, I SHALL NOT MOVE FROM THIS SEAT TILL I FIND A WAY TO END SORROW.
VISIONS OF THE LIFE OF PLEASURE FLOATED BEFORE HIS EYES. BUT NOTHING COULD TEMPT HIM.
AND THEN HE SAW LIGHT.
SIDDHARTHA BECAME THE BUDDHA, THE ENLIGHTENED ONE.
I KNOW. I KNOW THE TRUTH NOW. THE WAY TO END SORROW IS FOUND.

The Teachings of Buddhism

In Buddhism, there are some truths or realities that define the 'spiritually worthy ones.' They are known as the 'Four Noble Truths'. They are supposedly the first teaching given by the Buddha. The foundation of Buddhism is deep-rooted in these truths.

They are:

- ***Dukkha:*** Suffering is a natural characteristic of existence in the world
- ***Samudaya:*** Can be defined as the origin of dukkha which happens due to desire or attachment
- ***Nirodha:*** This dukkha can be stopped by completely letting go of desire or attachment
- ***Magga:*** Stands for the Eightfold Path, which will lead to letting go of the desire and attachment. Thus, ending the individual's dukkha

Upon viewing these truths symbolically, you will realise that they actually represent the Buddha's awakening. It is also an invitation for all those who wish to follow his path to attain the same spiritual experience as him.

In the Theravada tradition of Buddhism, the four truths grew to be of central importance. However, they do not hold the same amount of importance in the Mahayana tradition.

Now you must be wondering what the Eightfold Path stands for? Simply put, all creatures are in an endless cycle of rebirth till they attain a form of nirvana. Nirvana is the state when a person has no suffering or desire, is released from the effects of karma and breaks the cycle of death and rebirth.

The Eightfold Path is a guide for individuals to break the painful cycle of rebirth and attain the form of nirvana. It is represented by the Wheel of Dhamma. As the name suggests, the Eightfold Path consists of eight practices. They are:

Right view

We must understand that all of our actions bear consequences and that death is certainly not the end. Our actions and beliefs have consequences after death.

Right resolve

It can also be called Right intention. To follow this path, one must give up their home and adopt a life of a monk who relies on alms for survival. At a basic level, this path requires one to be harmless and refrain from ill will. At a deeper level, this path makes one think of how suffering is never permanent. Suffering comes and goes.

Right speech

As the name suggests, the individual must not lie or engage in rude speech. It also talks about how one mustn't tell one person what another says about them to cause disharmony or cracks in their relationship.

Right conduct

This path can also be referred to as Right action. It requires an individual to not kill or injure another being. It also talks about not stealing someone else's possessions and rejecting desires.

Right livelihood

One must only possess that which is required to sustain life. One should also lose their pride and beg for their food from others.

Right effort

As per this path, one must keep away from undesirable thoughts, doubts and any form of ill will. The path clears up the mind to practise one's work with a clear mind.

Right mindfulness

This path requires the individual never to be absent-minded and be conscious of what one is doing. One must always be mindful of the teachings that are important to the Buddhist path. This ensures the awareness of the temporariness of the body, feeling and mind.

Right concentration

Also known as Right *samadhi*. The word samadhi roughly means 'to collect' or 'to bring together'. Thus, it is often translated as 'concentration' or 'unification of the mind'. This path focuses on meditation and working towards the development of the Seven Factors of Awakening (Mindfulness, Investigation, Energy, Joy, Relaxation, Concentration and Equanimity)

The Eight Fold Path is often categorised into three divisions. They are:

Moral virtue: Right speech, Right action, Right livelihood

Meditation: Right effort, Right mindfulness, Right concentration

Insight, Wisdom: Right view, Right resolve

Gautama Buddha's teachings attracted all kinds of people. One reason was that he preached exclusively in Pali, the language of the people. Most Buddhist canons were written in Pali. In today's time, Pali is a forgotten language–it is studied to understand Buddhist scriptures.

A core belief of Gautama Buddha's teachings renounced the caste system. Several merchants from that period did not like that Brahmins and Kshatriyas claimed to be superior to them. Buddha welcomed everyone irrespective of their caste or wealth.

Some of his disciples were Upali, a barber who belonged to the lowest caste and Sunita, a sweeper. The richest man in the town of Sravasti, Anathapindika was also one of the Buddha's disciples. He even built the first

Buddhist monastery, which is a place of worship for Buddhists. Monasteries are a special place for Buddhists to focus on a simpler, less worldly life.

Gautama Buddha passed away approximately in the year 483 BCE. However, the followers of Buddhism only increased over time.

Buddhist texts are incredibly important to understand the period of history. They lend a lot of light to the Mahajanapadas. The Pali Canon, for example, are a collection of the Buddha's sermons and also incorporates speeches from some of his followers. There is also the Jatakas, stories from all of the Buddha's reincarnations.

PRACTISING BUDDHISM

WHILE WORSHIPPING IN A TEMPLE IS NOT MANDATORY, BUDDHISTS VISIT SHRINES TO MEDITATE WITH OTHER BUDDHISTS.

The first Buddhist shrines were stupas or ten dome-shaped mounds. They signified the Buddha's ashes. Later, more stupas were built to hold other sacred items. These stupas are mostly bell-shaped. To pay their respects to the Buddha, visitors walk around the stupas.

Japanese and Chinese Buddhists build towers with several tiers. They are known as pagodas. There have mainly five tiers representing the five elements of the Universe—earth, fire, wind, water and emptiness.

Often, Buddhists go on pilgrimages to places that were significant in Buddha's life. For example, Lumbini Grove, his birthplace, Bodh Gaya, the place of enlightenment, Sarnath, the venue of his first sermon and Kusinara, where he died.

The Buddha's teachings have been passed down by generations. A closer look at the core centre of his teachings should influence us to be more compassionate towards others. In today's time,

Buddhism has branched out to many different traditions. We have already discussed Theravada, Mahayana and Tibetan Buddhism. But did you know there is also Nichiren Buddhism, based on the teachings of a Japanese priest. Apart from that, there is also Western Buddhism and Navayana Buddhism.

Quiz

1) What are the two central philosophies of Buddhists?
2) Name the three types of Buddhism.
3) Where did the Buddha gain enlightenment?

Reflect

There is much to reflect on when one thinks about Buddhism. But central to it is the fact that dukkha is not permanent, but also a fact a life. Yes, sorrow will strike when it has to, but it will also pass. Is that a thought that you are comfortable with?

JAINISM

YOU KNOW KIDS, THERE WAS ANOTHER RELIGION BORN DURING THE TIME OF THE MAHAJANAPADAS—JAINISM. IT WAS A REACTION TO THE BRAHMANICAL TRADITIONS IN THE IRON AGE.

OVERVIEW

Just like Buddhism, Jainism is another ancient religion. It teaches liberation and bliss by living a life without harming anyone and leaving worldly pleasures or renunciation. In its essence, Jainism is about the welfare of every single being in the universe, no matter how big or small. It treats everyone and everything as significant. It also preaches the welfare for the health of the universe. There are three guiding principles upon which Jainism is based. They are:

- ***Samyak darshana* (correct perception):** Requires the individual to avoid assumptions to see clearly.
- ***Samyak jnana* (correct knowledge):** Requires the individual to have complete understanding of the Jain scriptures.
- ***Samyak charitra* (correct conduct):** Requires the individual to live a life of non-violence, avoid harming living things, being open-minded and free from any possessions whatsoever.

BUT DADI, HOW DID JAINISM COME ABOUT? WAS IT FOUNDED BY ONE PERSON, LIKE BUDDHISM?
AH, GOOD QUESTION, KID. LET'S FIND OUT!

There are two main branches of Jainism—*Svetambara* and *Digambra*. Svetambara means 'white-clad' and refers to the practice of wearing white clothes. Digambara are 'sky-clad' Jains and they believe in being naked and renouncing all worldly connections.

Unlike other religions, Jainism doesn't have a founder as such. Rather, the truth has been revealed several times by a tirthankara. A tirthankara is a teacher who shows the way. In other religions, a tirthankara is usually referred to as a 'prophet'.

Tirthankaras are teachers who have accomplished a spiritual goal of existence of the highest order. They then proceed to teach others how to achieve it and proceed on the way to liberation. The first Tirthankara was Rishabhanatha. The Jain texts credit him with introducing people to the first essential professions—writing, agriculture, knowledge, trade, crafts, and swordsmanship meant for self-defence.

Tirthankaras are not an incarnation of God. They weren't the founders of any religion either. Instead, they are ordinary souls that are born as humans. They attain the Tirthankara state through intense practices of penance, equanimity and meditation. They aren't avatars but people with a more developed form of the soul.

According to Jain mythology, they lived at various periods in history. Each one of them taught the same basic principles of Jain philosophy. However, they modify the Jain way of life, slightly, as per the culture and age in which they teach.

While there is little to no evidence for the existence of most of them, as per the Jains, there are 24 tirthankaras of the 'present age'. They are: *Adinatha, Ajita, Sambhava, Abhinandana, Sumati, Padmaprabha, Suparshva, Chandraprabha, Suvidhi, Shital, Shreyansa, Vasupujya, Vimala, Ananta, Dharma, Shanti, Kunthu, Ara, Malli, Muni Suvrata, Nami, Nemi, Parshva and Mahavira*.

As per Svetambara Jains, tirthankaras can either be a man or a woman. This is why they believe that the tirthankara called Malli was a princess. However, Digambar Jains strongly believe that women cannot be tirthankaras and argue that Malli was actually a man.

QUIZ

1) Name the two types of Jainism.
2) What is a thirthankara?
3) How many thirthankaras have there been in our age?

REFLECT

Thirthankaras, according to Jain lore, are normal people who attain a higher level of existence through practice, meditation and equanimity. Is that something you can strive towards? To try and find a path that is of interest to you?

MAHAVIRA

BUT NOW, LET'S FOCUS ON ONE TIRTHANKARA IN PARTICULAR— THE TWENTY-FOURTH TIRTHANKARA, MAHAVIRA. HAVE YOU HEARD ABOUT HIM, KIDS?

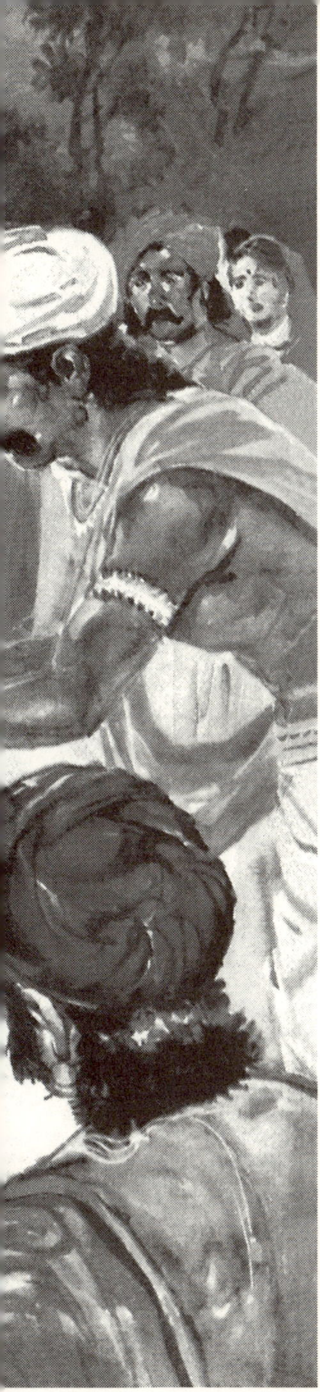

The word 'Mahavira' originates from the words *'maha,'* meaning great and *'vir,'* meaning hero. Mahavira is considered to be the man who shaped Jainism into its present-day form. However, he is sometimes wrongly called 'the founder of Jainism.' He is only the world's most recent tirthankara. He is also the last tirthankara of this age. It is more valuable to view him as someone who reformed and popularised the ancient faith and not its founder.

Mahavira was born as Vardhamana in north-east India in approximately 599 BCE. He was the son of King Siddhartha and Queen Trishala.

They were members of the warrior Kshatriya caste and followed the teachings of Parshva, the twenty-third tirthankara. It is said that before the birth of Vardhamana, Queen Trishala had some strange dreams. The King then called for astrologers who predicted that the Queen will give birth to a child who is destined to be great. Vardhamana was a bright child. He mastered knowledge with complete ease to such an extent that even his gurus were amazed.

AFTER VARDHAMANA WAS BORN, THE KING THREW A FEAST THAT LASTED FOR TEN DAYS. THE ENTIRE KINGDOM REJOICED AND CELEBRATED. TALK ABOUT A GRAND BIRTHDAY PARTY!

Our childhoods are filled with adventures that we cherish for all our lives. Vardhamana, too, had incidents from his childhood that would become lessons of tranquillity and compassion.

As a child, Vardhamana was calm, brave and composed. One day, he was playing with his friends when one of them screamed, 'Ah! Cobra! Run!' All the other boys got startled and ran for their lives. However, Vardhamana was patient. He wasn't bothered by the snake's presence. When the Cobra came near him, Vardhamana bent towards it. His friends started panicking and asked him to move away. However, Vardhamana decidedly proceeded to caress the snake. The snake hissed, but then suddenly, a somewhat agitated snake had been pacified.
It calmly disappeared into the woods after that. Vardhamana's friends were so impressed, they raised him on their shoulders and celebrated his bravery.

When Vardhamana was a young man, he was roaming markets in the city of Kundagram when suddenly he heard a scream. 'RUN FOR YOUR LIVES!' screamed a merchant. There was chaos everywhere. Shops were in a complete mess, and everyone was running helter-skelter. An elephant had gone berserk and was causing damage everywhere.

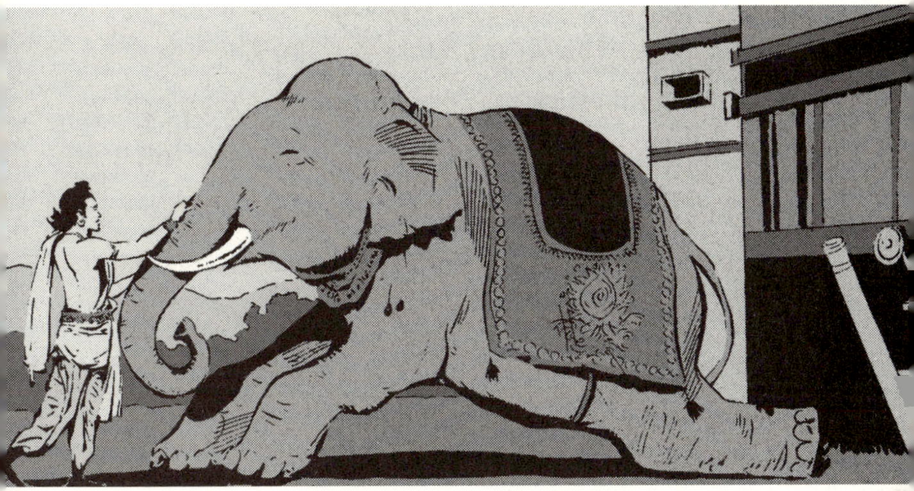

Vardhamana decided to put an end to this. He walked towards the elephant and boldly stood in front of it. The furious elephant was about to attack Vardhamana when Vardhamana touched it. By his mere touch, the elephant calmed down completely. The rampaging elephant could be seen gently bowing down on its knees in front of the prince. Once the elephant was calm, people started gathering around. At first they just looked at the prince in awe. They then started celebrating him. 'We thought we were dead for sure!' said one merchant. 'You are a saviour. What you did was impossible. We are forever grateful,' said a mother with a newborn baby.

Vardhamana's father passed away, and he craved freedom from worldly attachments. He was thirty years old when he decided to leave everything and go out in search of the truth. He wandered from place to place. He did not stay for more than a day in a village, and more than five days in a town, throughout his journey. Eventually, he discarded clothes and strictly practised penance and austerity for twelve years.

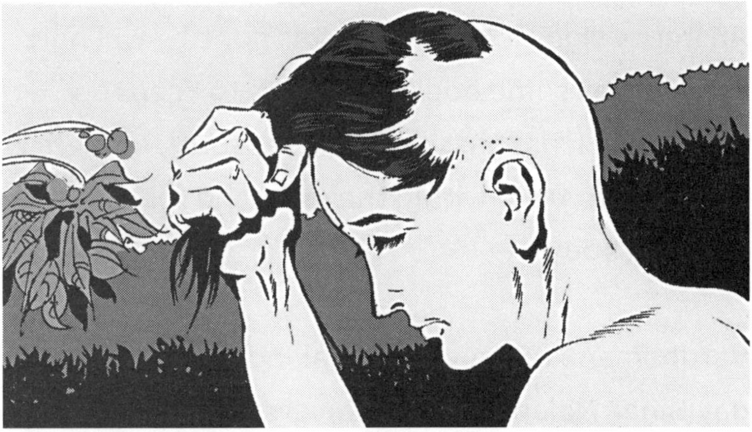

Austerity signifies restraint. It is done by willingly giving away some bodily comforts to keep the mind away from passions and pleasures. Austerity can be both from within the mind and for the external body.

Vardhamana often visited Nalanda in present-day Bihar. Nalanda was a university that focussed on studying religious texts for a better understanding of life. It is said that Mahavira spent fourteen monsoons at Nalanda. During one such visit, he met a sage called Gosala Makkhalipuuta. Impressed by Mahavira's knowledge, Gosala decided to become his

disciple and live with him for six years. However, they started having different opinions on the topic of rejuvenation. Eventually, Gosala left to establish a new religious order known as Ajivikas.

After twelve years of continuous penance, Vardhamana meditated under a tree beside the river Rijjupalika. At the age of 42, Vardhamana attained supreme wisdom, also known as *Keval Jnana,* outside the town of Jrimbhikgram in Bihar. He then came to be known as Mahavira or the great hero. He was also known as *Jina* or 'the conqueror'. Another name for him was *Kevalin.*

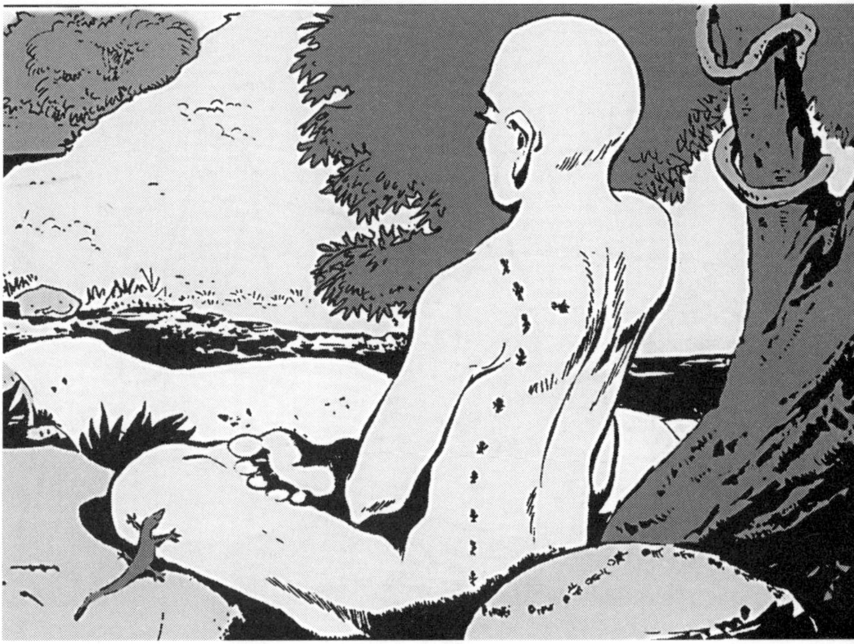

His followers were called *nirgranthas* which meant that they were free from bonds. His preachings came to be known as Jainism.

Mahavir's followers began imitating his behaviour. He welcomed all, regardless of their caste, to his sangha. Once, one of his followers, a wealthy man, was greeted by an outcast beggar. The beggar pleaded, 'O kind sir, please feed me. I am hungry.' The man happily invited him into his house. However, his wife called him aside and questioned his behaviour. She said, 'Have you gone crazy?! Why are you feeding this outcast?' The man replied, 'If Mahavir can admit an outcast into his sangha then the least we can do is feed one.'

At approximately 527 BCE in Pava, Bihar, Mahavir breathed his last.

QUIZ

1) What was Mahavira's first name?
2) For how long did Mahavira wander from place to place?
3) What is austerity?

REFLECT

What is inspirational about the life of Mahavira? Is it his ability to identify with animals and humans alike? Was it the fact that he spent so much time trying to seek knowledge? Could you sacrifice everything for a higher purpose?

THE TENETS

KIDS, DID YOU KNOW, JAINS STRONGLY BELIEVE IN THE CONCEPT OF REINCARNATION? THEY BELIEVE THAT THEIR SOULS ARE UNIQUE SUBSTANCES IN THE VAST UNIVERSE.

Jains believe that the soul takes the form of different living beings. This cycle is in the form of birth, death, rebirth. It is continuous since the universe has no beginning or end. However, the end goal is for the individual to get rid of the karma on their soul. It leads to the termination of this cycle. As soon as this goal is reached, the individual's soul attains all knowledge and rests forever in heaven. This is Nirvana.

Do you know what karma is? In case you don't, it's the theory that every action has a consequence. Simply put, it's the law of cause and effect but specifically for the soul. Jainism is quite an intricate and well-detailed religion. Jainism talks about karma and the cycle of rebirth. However, it also gives solutions by guiding the individual on how to get rid of it.

There are a set of rules in different religions. Just like how Christianity has the Ten Commandments and Buddhism has certain principles. Jains uphold the following principles

by keeping non-violence in thought, deed and action and by being vegetarians:

Ahimsa: To protect all life

Satya: To always speak the truth

Asteya: To never steal

Brahmacharya: To not commit adultery

Aparigraha: To limit the possessions one has

Fasting is very common in Jainism. It is intense and to the point where some individuals fast to death because they would rather die than bring any harm to plant life.

Apart from that, Jains also perform their sacred rituals at a temple or a *derasar*. The rituals are as follows:

Puja

It is concentrating on the soul through prayer. It is often practised in the presence of sculptures of the teachers. These sculptures help individuals be guided to attain moksha, or liberation. Moksha is attained when an individual enters a different state of the soul which is now free from any karmic influences and their sins are forgiven.

Samayik

A 48-minute ritual that makes an individual seek forgiveness for their sins.

Namokar Mantra

It is a short prayer that shows respect towards the perfect souls that have achieved nirvana. It can be said at any time.

Now you know so much about Jainism. Let's familiarise ourselves with a few more unique concepts about the religion.

Holy Week

Jains observe the holy week (eight to ten days) of Paryushan where they reflect upon their actions throughout the past year. This week takes place in August or September and is the biggest event in the Jain calendar. It concludes with a 3-hour prayer called *pratikraman*.

No Gods

Jainism is neither created by nor is relies on any gods. They do not believe in any spiritual beings. It is a religion that is built on the principles of self-reliance.

Deadly Sins

Just like how Christianity has the Seven Deadly Sins, Jainism recognises four sins. They are known as *kashaya*. They are anger, pride, greed and deceit.

Six eternal substances

According to Jainism, the universe is composed of six eternal substances or dravyas. They are living and non-living entities. The living entity is the soul or the jiva. The non-living entities are *pudgala* (matter), *dharma* (motion), *adharma* (rest), *akasa* (space), and *kala* (time).

Seven *tattva*

Tattva or fundamental truths constitute reality.

The seven tattvas are:

- The soul.
- The non-soul.
- The influx of matter into the soul.
- Mixing of the soul and karmas.
- Obstruction of matter into the soul.
- The gradual dissociation of karmic matter from the soul moksha.

Eight practices

Jainism has several practices to support the *mahavratas*. They are meditation, festivals, rituals, fasting, prayers, vegetarianism, monasticism, and pilgrimages.

Did you know? Jains believe in multi-universes and that people can be reborn in any one of the three universes. We are in Bharat Kshetra.

Jainism spread rapidly during Mahavira's lifetime. However, even after his death, it spread considerably. Let's look at some of the reasons for the widespread practice of Jainism.

When simple language is used to communicate, the masses respond well. Mahavira used a common dialect instead of Sanskrit while preaching. Sanskrit, at the time, was considered the language of the intellectuals. The languages he used were colloquial languages—The language of the Madaghi and Prakrit people.

There was also royal patronage which played an important factor in the spread of Jainism. Mahavir was born to a Kshatriya family. The Kshatriya kings were tired of Brahmin supremacy. Due to this, they embraced Jainism. Jainism was patronised by the rulers of Magadha, Ajatasatru and his successor Udayin.

The first Emperor of Ancient India and the founder of the Maurya Empire, Chandragupta Maurya played a major role in spreading Jainism across Karnataka.

In the 4th and 1st Century BCE, Jainism also spread to Kalinga. There, it received the patronage of King Kharavela of the Chedi dynasty. Later, it spread to Gujarat, Malwa and Rajasthan. In today's time, Jains are mainly engaged in trade and commerce.

Jain monks also help spread Jainism. They visited several places and had intellectual discussions giving people a glimpse of their simplicity and influence. Jain saint Bhadrabahu also helped spread Jainism in the 4th Century BCE.

Finally, Jainism was also popularised by the writings of Gunabhadra, Haribhadra, Hemachandra and Ravikirti. They managed to influence people into accepting Jainism.

Today, the majority of Jains reside in India. However, with only 4-5 million followers worldwide, Jainism is a small religion. As of today, there are over 100,000 Jains living in the United States of America. Jainism is rapidly spreading in Japan, where around 5000 families have converted to Jainism in the last decade.

Jains also form one of the wealthiest communities in India. Jains are also regarded as intellectual people. Their literacy in India has exceeded over 97 per cent.

Even Mahatma Gandhi, the Father of our Nation, was highly influenced by Jainism. He believed that no other religion managed to explain the concept of *ahimsa,* or non-violence, like Jainism.

Today, there are Jain temples all around India. These include the Ranakpur Jain Temple in Rajasthan, the Gomateshwara Temple in Karnataka, Palitana Temples in Gujarat, Sri Digambar Jain Lal Mandir in Delhi, Sonagiri Temple in Madhya Pradesh and Shikharji Temple in Jharkhand.

Even in today's time, Jainism has essential and significant teachings. For example, the

Jainism principle of *aparigraha* refers to not taking more than what is necessary to live. On a small scale, this means refraining oneself from overconsumption of food and energy. On a larger scale, it refers to deforestation and exploitation of nature. So, you see, in a way, Jainism had already commented about climate change years before anyone thought that it was even a threat.

It can be noted that while the teachings of Jainism are close to both Buddhism and Hinduism, Jainism stands apart with its views on non-violence, looking at the world from various perspectives, and having no attachment whatsoever to earthly possessions.

While these texts have been around since the second century BCE, they still continue to teach us a lot about compassion and the circle of life. We, too, can implement the basic teachings of Jainism in our day-to-day lives.

Perhaps the first step to peace is to follow the path of non-violence. Non-violence begins from the stage where one doesn't have any ill will towards those around them. Jainism even has the principle of *ahimsa paramo dharma*, which states that non-violence isn't only confined to refraining from being violent. But, it also requires an individual to show love and care towards other human beings. You know what they say, charity begins at home!

QUIZ

1) Where do a majority of Jains reside today?
2) What did Mahatma Gandhi believe about Jainism?
3) Can you name two major Jain temples?

REFLECT

Non-violence was a political tool used by Mahatma Gandhi to win India's freedom. It is also a way of life for the Jains. What do you think about non-violence? Now that you have read about both Buddhism and Jainism, do you think you can incorporate some of your new learnings to your daily life?

THE MAHAJANAPADAS

Mahājanapadas and janapadas

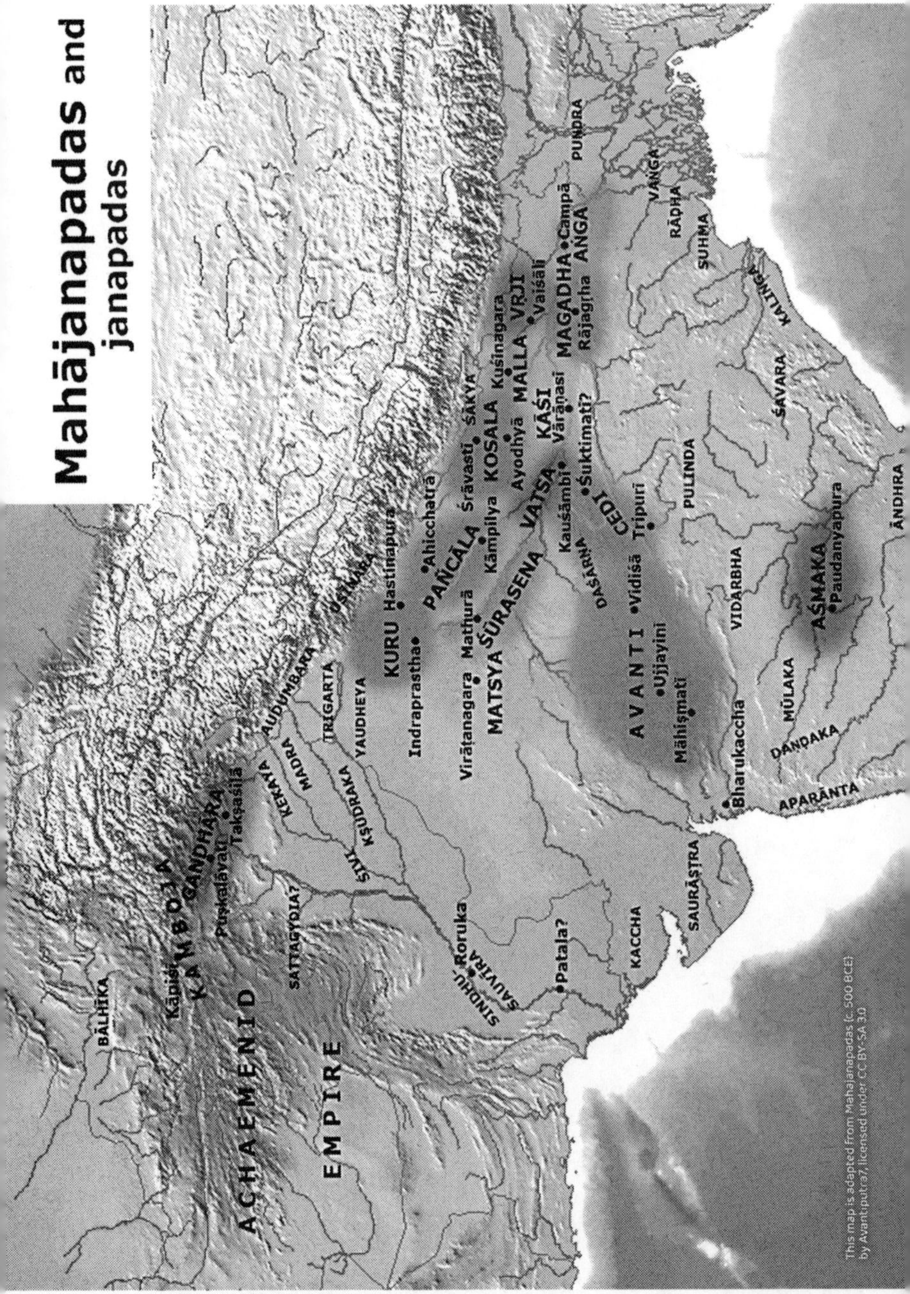

This map is used for representational purpose only.

Anga

One of the oldest Mahajanapadas, it is mentioned in various texts. It was a great trade and commerce centre due to its proximity to the sea.

Assaka

A southern Mahajanapada, it included areas in present-day Andhra Pradesh, Telangana and Maharashtra, along the banks of the Godavari.

Avanti

Along with Kosala, Vatsa and Magadha, Avanti was one of the four greatest monarchies of the era. With the river Narmada running right through it, it was one of the most important western kingdoms. Its capital was Ujjaini, and stood in present-day Madhya Pradesh.

Chedi

Another kingdom in present-day Madhya Pradesh, the Chedis are some of the oldest tribes to form a Mahajanapadas. They even find mention in the Rigveda!

Gandhara

The Gandharis were another ancient people, mentioned as early as the Rigvedas, and again as allies of the Kurus in the Mahabharata. They were first located in the northwest, in eastern Afghanistan and Punjab. As the Iron Age wore on, they shifted eastward, and their final capital was in Taxila in present-day Pakistan.

Kamboja

Another northern territory, the Kambojans were most likely one of the Mahajanapadas that was a republic. Even the Mahabharata and Ashokan edicts much later mention Kamboja as a republic, even though some Buddhist texts might contradict this.

Kashi

Possibly the most prominent of the early Mahajanapadas, Kashi was situated in present-day Uttar Pradesh, with their capital in Varanasi. During the time of the Buddha, Kashi was conquered by Kosala.

Kosala

With its capital in Ayodhya, the Kosala state has an important place in history. The most famous of their princes, of course, was Lord Rama. Located in central and eastern Uttar Pradesh, Kosala was another ancient tribe that finds mention in the Veda and the Epics.

Kuru

Again, famous for their role in the Mahabharata, the Kuru clan's capital was Indraprastha. This is in and around present-day Delhi.

Magadha

The most prosperous of the Mahajanapadas, Magadha was located in present-day Bihar. Its capital was Pataliputra, or Patna as it is known today. Standing in the confluence of the rivers, Ganga, Son, Punpun and Gandak, with the mines of Jharkhand and Bihar just a few hours away,

Magadha became one of the richest and most powerful states in the period. Magadha was the state of Bimbisara, who gave shelter and befriended the Buddha.

Malla

Malla in present-day Uttar Pradesh was where both the Buddha and Mahavira took their last meals and attained moksha. Malla was one of the states that was run as a republic during the time.

Matsya

Located in modern-day Rajasthan, close to Jaipur, the Matsyas called Viratanagara their capital.

Panachala

Panchala was divided into two territories, north and south. In modern-day Uttar Pradesh, Adhichhatra served as the capital of the north and Chhatravati for the south. Originally a kingdom, Panchala might have switched to a republican form of government around 600 BCE.

Surasena

Located, again, in present-day Uttar Pradesh, Surasena was a prominent Mahajanapada. Its capital was in Mathura. Its king, Avantiputra, was one of the Buddha's first disciples. Buddhism spread very quickly in the region. Surasena was also a republic at this time.

Vajji

Also known as Vrijji, with Vaishali as capital, in present-day Bihar, Vajji became one of the most prominent Buddhist Mahajanpadas after the Buddha's passing.

Vatsa

Another extremely prosperous Mahajanapada was Vatsa, with its capital in Kausambi. Located near present-day Allahabad, this was a Mahajanapada that was home to many extremely wealthy merchants and traders.

QUIZ

1) Name the oldest Mahajanapadas.
2) Which was the most prosperous of the Mahajanapadas?
3) Name the Mahajanapada connected to Lord Rama.

REFLECT

We are at the end of our journey. Think about all the achievements of Indians during the Iron Age. We developed new religions and new ways of agriculture, we revolutionised the way we live and how we pray. It was a wonderful era in our history, full of progress, movement and opening of new horizons. How does the Iron Age impact your life? Do you think if we skipped one major step in our evolution, your life would be completely different?

AND THAT, KIDS, WAS THE STORY OF THE IRON AGE IN INDIA. WHAT DO YOU GUYS THINK?
THAT WAS STUNNING, DADI. WE PROGRESSED SO MUCH DURING THIS TIME.

YA, DADI. WHAT I WOULD DO TO SIT IN ON ONE OF THOSE KAUTUHAL SABHA MEETINGS!
AND A SERMON FROM MAHAVIRA OR THE BUDDHA!

BUT DADI, IS THIS STORY OVER?
YA! I WANT MORE. WHAT HAPPENED NEXT?

KIDS, I COULD TELL YOU STORIES FROM INDIAN HISTORY FOR ALL MY LIFE AND THEY STILL WOULDN'T BE OVER. BUT RIGHT NOW, YOU GUYS HAVE REALLY WORN ME OUT. SO CAN I MAKE A DEAL?

THE NEXT TIME I WILL TELL YOU ABOUT ALEXANDER AND HIS VISIT TO INDIA! AND I'LL TELL YOU ABOUT SOME OF THE GREATEST KINGDOMS INDIA HAS EVER KNOWN! BUT I NEED TO BRUSH UP MY HISTORY BEFORE THAT. SO YOU MUST JOIN ME NEXT TIME!

The red panda is a reddish brown mammal with a long, ringed tail and a raccoon-like face. This endangered animal is found in the forests of eastern Himalayas and is the state animal of Sikkim. Also called firefox, the cat-sized animal is largely herbivores but also eats insects. The red panda uses its bushy tail to balance and wrap it around its body to stay warm in the chilly mountains. A victim of deforestation, there are less than 10,000 animals remaining in the wild.